Earth

by
Christine Taylor-Butler

Children's Press
An Imprint of Scholastic Inc.
New York Toronto London Auckland Sydney
Mexico City New Delhi Hong Kong
Danbury, Connecticut

These content vocabulary word builders
are for grades 1–2.

Consultant: Michelle Yehling, Astronomy Education Consultant

Photo Credits:

Photographs © 2008: Corbis Images: 4 bottom left, 4 top, 11 (Matthias Kulka), 17 (Jim Sugar); Hawaii Volcanoes National Park via SODA: 4 bottom right, 15; NASA: back cover; Peter Arnold Inc./Astrofoto: 5 bottom right, 9 top; Photo Researchers, NY: cover (European Space Agency/SPL), 1, 5 bottom left, 5 top left, 9 bottom (Mehau Kulyk); PhotoDisc/Getty Images via SODA: 2, 5 top right, 7, 23; U.S. Department of Agriculture via SODA: 19.

Illustration Credits:

Illustration page 13 by Bernard Adnet.

Illustration pages 20–21 by Greg Harris.

Book Design: SimonSays Design!
Book Production: The Design Lab

Library of Congress Cataloging-in-Publication Data
Taylor-Butler, Christine.
Earth / by Christine Taylor-Butler.—Updated ed.
   p. cm.—(Scholastic news nonfiction readers)
Includes bibliographical references and index.
ISBN-13: 978-0-531-22625-4
ISBN-10: 0-531-22625-5
1. Earth—Juvenile literature. I. Title.
QE501.T35 2007
550—dc22   2006102767

1 2 3 4 5 6 7 8 9 10 R 17 16 15 14 13 12 11 10 09 08

CONTENTS

WORD HUNT

Look for these words as you read. They will be in **bold**.

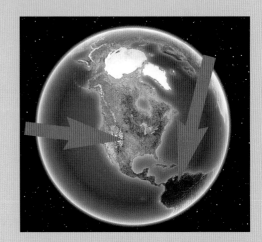

continents
(**kon**-tih-nuhnts)

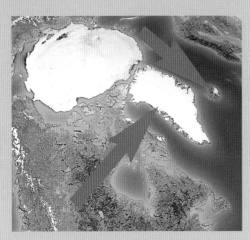

islands
(**eye**-luhndz)

lava
(**lah**-vuh)

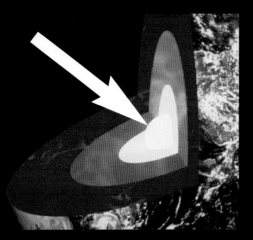

core
(kor)

Earth
(urth)

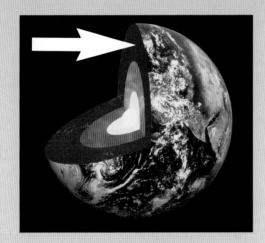

mantle
(**man**-tuhl)

solar system
(**soh**-lur **siss**-tuhm)

Earth!

You can eat the crust of a piece of bread.

But can you eat the crust of **Earth**?

No. Earth's crust is made of rock.

Most of Earth's crust is covered with water.

Earth is the third planet from the Sun.

Earth is the only planet in the **solar system** with human life.

The crust is one of Earth's layers. It is the outside layer.

The **mantle** is under the crust.

The **core** is in the center of Earth.

solar system

Earth

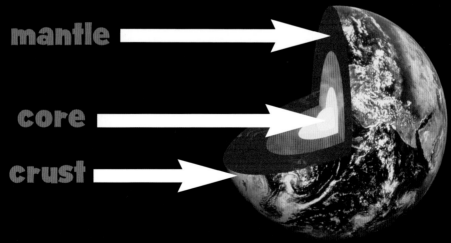

mantle

core

crust

Earth's crust is more than 40 miles
(64.5 kilometers) thick in some places.

Large parts of Earth's crust rise above the water.

These parts are called **continents**.

Smaller parts rise above water, too.

These parts are called **islands**.

People live on continents and islands.

island

continent

Earth has seven continents and many islands. This continent is North America.

Earth's crust is broken into many pieces, called plates.

These are not like dinner plates.

These plates are made of rock.

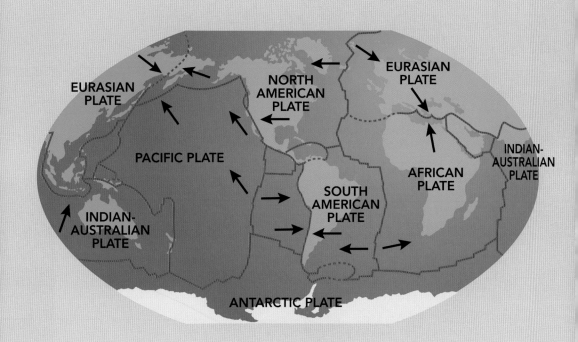

EURASIAN PLATE

NORTH AMERICAN PLATE

EURASIAN PLATE

PACIFIC PLATE

INDIAN-AUSTRALIAN PLATE

SOUTH AMERICAN PLATE

AFRICAN PLATE

INDIAN-AUSTRALIAN PLATE

ANTARCTIC PLATE

The red lines show the shapes of Earth's plates.

Earth's mantle is under the crust.

It is made of melted rock called magma.

Earth's plates float on the magma.

Magma that comes out of Earth's crust is called **lava**.

lava

Hot lava can glow red.

Earth's plates move.

Sometimes this creates earthquakes.

Sometimes the crust pushes up.

This creates mountains.

Sometimes magma rises.

This creates a volcano.

Lava shoots out of this volcano.

We eat things that live on Earth's crust.

We eat things that grow in Earth's crust.

But we don't eat Earth's crust!

Corn is one food that grows on Earth's crust.

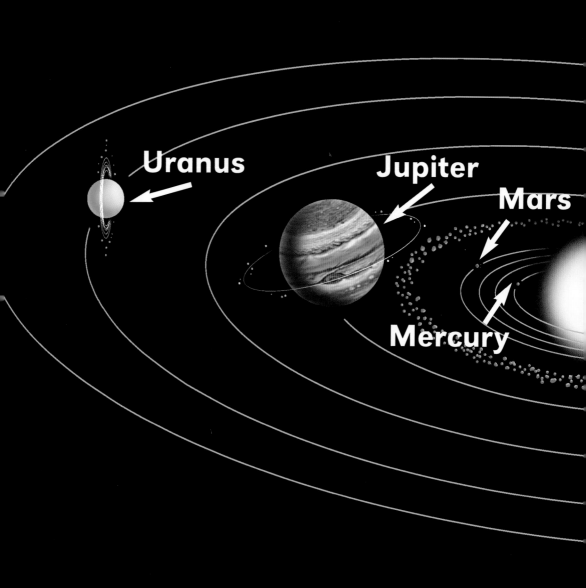

Uranus

Jupiter

Mars

Mercury

EARTH

IN OUR SOLAR SYSTEM

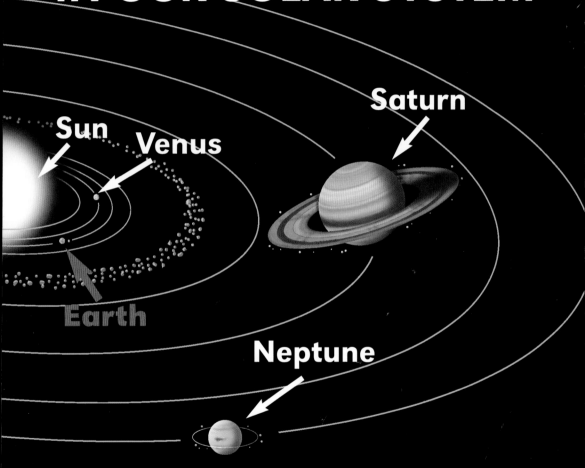

Sun

Venus

Saturn

Earth

Neptune

YOUR NEW WORDS

continents (**kon**-tih-nuhnts) very large areas of land; there are seven continents on Earth

core (kor) the center of Earth

Earth (urth) the planet we live on

islands (**eye**-luhndz) small areas of land that rise above the water

lava (**lah**-vuh) hot magma that comes out of a volcano

mantle (**man**-tuhl) the layer between Earth's crust and the core

solar system (**soh**-lur **siss**-tuhm) the group of planets, moons, and other things that travel around the Sun

Earth Is an Amazing Planet!

A year is how long it takes a planet to go around the Sun.
1 Earth year=365 days

A day is how long it takes a planet to turn one time.
1 Earth day = 24 hours

Earth has 1 moon.

Earth is more than 4 billion years old.

Earth is the only planet in the solar system with liquid water on its surface.

INDEX

FIND OUT MORE

Book:

Luhr, James F., ed. *Smithsonian Earth.* New York: DK Publishing, Inc., 2003.

Web site:

Solar System Exploration
http://sse.jpl.nasa.gov/planets

MEET THE AUTHOR

Christine Taylor-Butler is the author of more than twenty books for children. She holds a degree in Engineering from M.I.T. She lives in Kansas City with her family where they have a telescope for searching the skies.

SCHOLASTIC News
Nonfiction Readers

Uranus

by
Christine Taylor-Butler

Children's Press
An Imprint of Scholastic Inc.
New York Toronto London Auckland Sydney
Mexico City New Delhi Hong Kong
Danbury, Connecticut

These content vocabulary word builders
are for grades 1–2.

Consultant: Michelle Yehling, Astronomy Education Consultant

Photo Credits:

Photographs © 2008: AP/Wide World Photos: cover; Getty Images/Antonio M. Rosario: 9; NASA: 4 bottom right, 5 top left, 15, 17 (JPL), back cover, 1, 2, 4 top, 5 bottom, 7, 13, 14, 19, 23 right; Photo Researchers, NY/Detlev van Ravenswaay: 4 bottom left; PhotoDisc/via SODA: 23 left.

Illustration Credits:

Diagram on pages 20–21 by Greg Harris   Illustration on page 5 and 11 by Pat Rasch

Book Design: SimonSays Design!
Book Production: The Design Lab

Library of Congress Cataloging-in-Publication Data
Taylor-Butler, Christine.
Uranus / by Christine Taylor-Butler.—Updated ed.
    p. cm.—(Scholastic news nonfiction readers)
Includes bibliographical references and index.
ISBN-13: 978-0-531-22632-2
ISBN-10: 0-531-22632-8
1. Uranus (Planet)—Juvenile literature. I. Title.
QB681.T39 2007
523.47—dc22   2006102777

All rights reserved. Published by Children's Press, an imprint of Scholastic Inc.
Published simultaneously in Canada. Printed in China.

SCHOLASTIC, CHILDREN'S PRESS, and associated logos are trademarks and/or registered trademarks of Scholastic Inc.

1 2 3 4 5 6 7 8 9 10 R 17 16 15 14 13 12 11 10 09 08

CONTENTS

WORD HUNT

Look for these words as you read. They will be in **bold**.

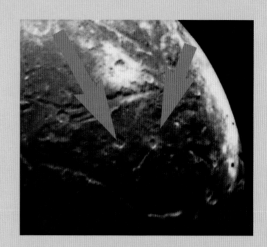

craters
(**kray**-turz)

solar system
(**soh**-lur **siss**-tuhm)

Titania
(tuh-**tane**-yuh)

4

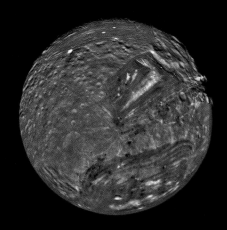

Miranda
(muh-**ran**-duh)

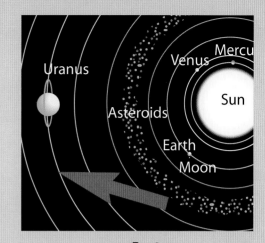

orbit
(**or**-bit)

Uranus
(**yur**-uh-nus)

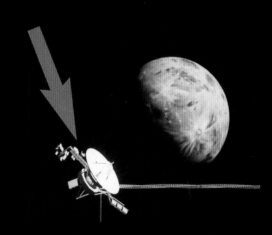

Voyager 2
(**voi**-ij-uhr 2)

5

Uranus!

Uranus has clouds of gas. The gas is very cold.

Closer to the planet the gas turns into icy slush.

7

Uranus is the seventh planet from the Sun.

Uranus is one of the biggest planets in our **solar system**.

Sun

Uranus

9

Uranus travels around the Sun on a path called an **orbit**.

Most planets also spin like tops along their orbits. But Uranus spins like a ball rolling.

Scientists think Uranus was hit by something that tipped it sideways.

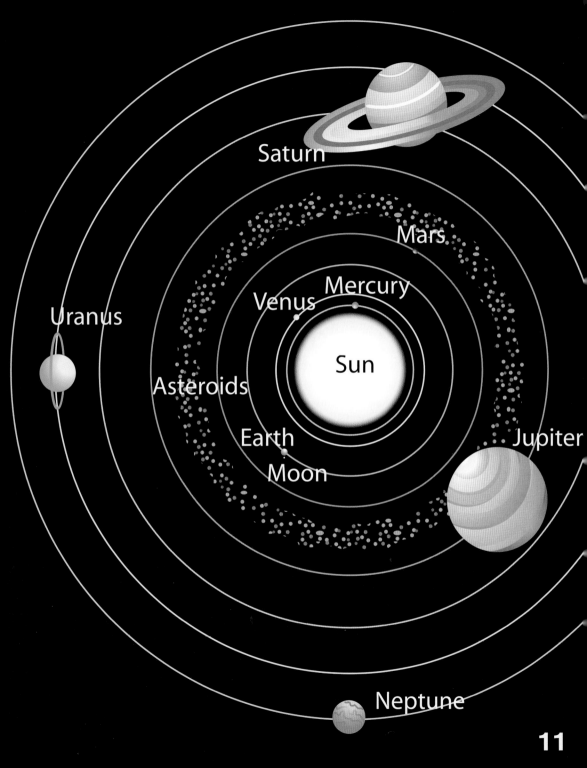

Saturn

Mars

Mercury

Venus

Uranus

Sun

Asteroids

Earth

Jupiter

Moon

Neptune

11

Uranus has 11 rings.

They are hard to see.

The rings on Uranus are made of ice. The ice is covered in dark dust.

13

Uranus has at least 27 moons.

The largest moon is **Titania**.

Titania has **craters**, like Earth's moon.

It also has long, deep marks that stretch around it.

crater

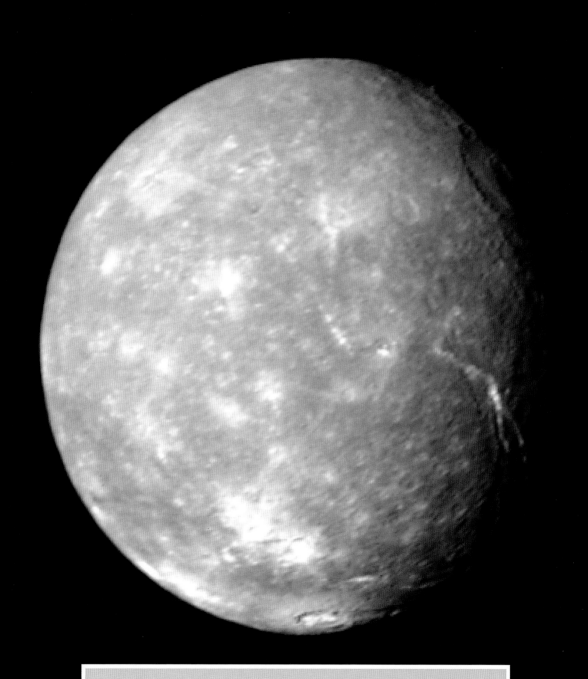

Titania was first seen in 1787.

Miranda is also one of Uranus's moons.

Miranda is one of the oddest worlds anywhere.

It has craters. It has long marks. It has broken rocks. It has giant cliffs.

Scientists know how Miranda got some marks, but they do not know about them all.

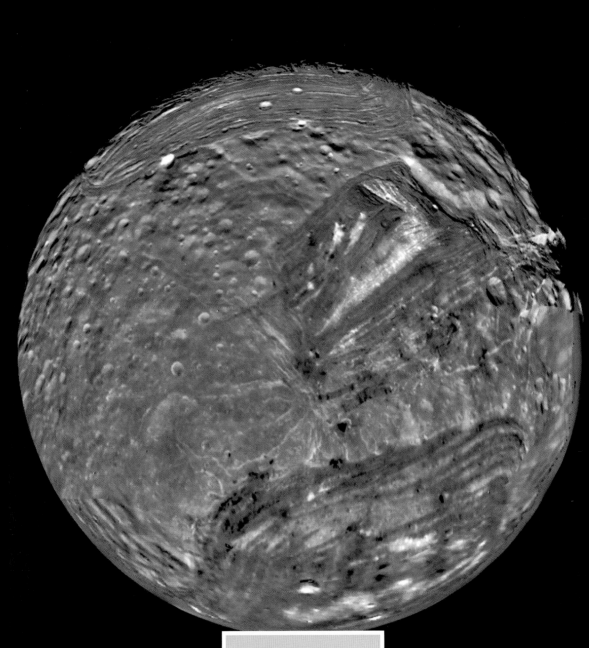

Miranda

Voyager 2 is a space probe.

It is the only craft to go near Uranus.

It is why we know more about this planet.

Thank you, *Voyager 2*!

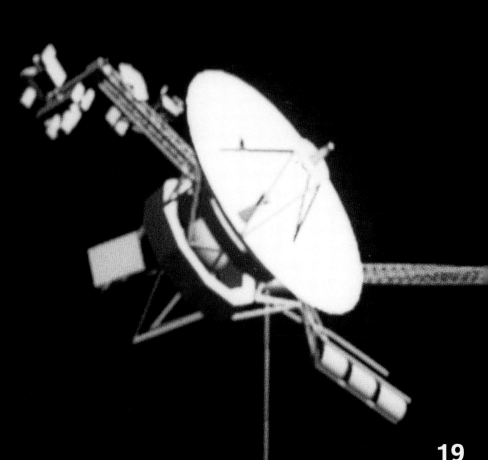

Voyager 2 first went into space in 1977.

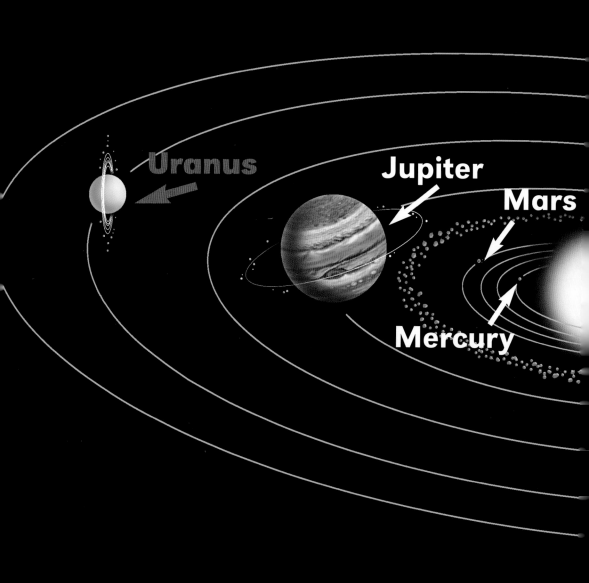

Uranus

Jupiter

Mars

Mercury

URANUS

IN OUR SOLAR SYSTEM

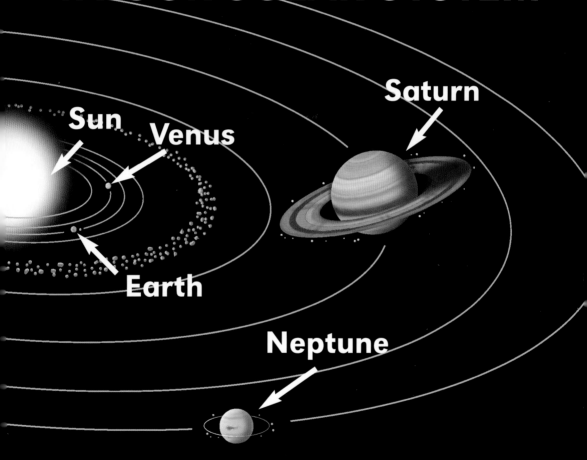

Saturn

Sun

Venus

Earth

Neptune

YOUR NEW WORDS

craters (**kray**-turz) large dents or holes in an object

Miranda (muh-**ran**-duh) one of Uranus's moons

orbit (**or**-bit) the path an object takes around another object

solar system (**soh**-lur **siss**-tuhm) the group of planets, moons, and other things that travel around the Sun

Titania (tuh-**tane**-yuh) Uranus's largest moon

Uranus (**yur**-uh-nus) a planet named after the Greek god of the sky

Voyager 2 (**voi**-ij-uhr 2) the first and only space probe to visit Uranus and Neptune

Earth and Uranus

A year is how long it takes a planet to go around the Sun.

 1 Earth year =365 days

 1 Uranus year =30,687 Earth days

A day is how long it takes a planet turn one time.

 1 Earth day = 24 hours

 1 Uranus day = 17 Earth hours

A moon is an object that circles around a planet.

 Earth has 1 moon.

 Uranus has at least 27 moons with more being found all the time.

Scientists do not agree on which way is North on Uranus.

23

INDEX

FIND OUT MORE
Book:
Burnham, Robert. *Children's Atlas of the Universe.* Pleasantville, NY:
Reader's Digest Children's Publishing, Inc., 2000.

Web site:
Solar System Exploration
http://sse.jpl.nasa.gov/planets

MEET THE AUTHOR
Christine Taylor-Butler is the author of more than
twenty books for children. She holds a degree in Engineering
from M.I.T. She lives in Kansas City with her family, where
they have a telescope for searching the skies.

SCHOLASTIC
News
Nonfiction Readers

Mercury

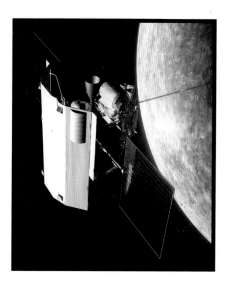

by
Christine Taylor-Butler

Children's Press
An Imprint of Scholastic Inc.
New York Toronto London Auckland Sydney
Mexico City New Delhi Hong Kong
Danbury, Connecticut

These content vocabulary word builders
are for grades 1–2.

Consultant: Michelle Yehling, Astronomy Education Consultant

Photo Credits:

Photographs © 2008: Finley Holiday Film: back cover; NASA: 5 top left, 15 top, 15 bottom, 17 (Jet Propulsion Laboratory), 1, 5 bottom right, 19 (John Hopkins University Applied Physics Laboratory/Carnegie Institution of Washington); Photo Researchers, NY: 11 (Chris Butler), 4 top, 13 (Lynette Cook), 4 bottom left, 14 (Ted Kinsman), 4 bottom right (David Nunuk/SPL), cover, 2, 5 top right, 7, 23 (U.S. Geological Survey/SPL), 5 bottom left, 9 (Detlev van Ravenswaay); PhotoDisc/Getty Images via SODA: 23 left.

Illustration Credit:

Illustration pages 20–21 by Greg Harris

Book Design: SimonSays Design!
Book Production: The Design Lab

Library of Congress Cataloging-in-Publication Data
Taylor-Butler, Christine.
Mercury / by Christine Taylor-Butler.—Updated ed.
    p. cm.—(Scholastic news nonfiction readers)
Includes bibliographical references and index.
ISBN-13: 978-0-531-22628-5
ISBN-10: 0-531-22628-X
1. Mercury (Planet)—Juvenile literature. I. Title.
QB611.T39 2007
523.41—dc22   2006102771

1 2 3 4 5 6 7 8 9 10 R   17 16 15 14 13 12 11 10 09 08

CONTENTS

WORD HUNT

Look for these words as you read. They will be in **bold**.

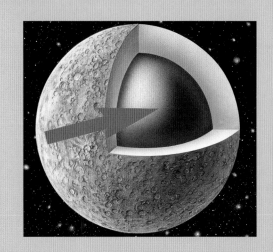

core
(kor)

meteorite
(**mee**-tee-ur-ite)

moon
(moon)

4

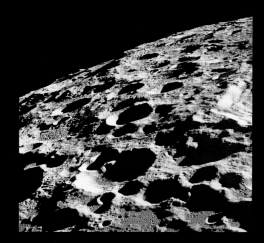

craters
(kray-turz)

Mercury
(muhr-kyur-ree)

solar system
(**soh**-lur **siss**-tuhm)

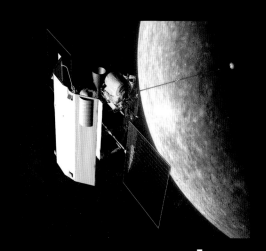

space probe
(spayss prohb)

Mercury!

Can you sing on **Mercury**?

No. You cannot sing on Mercury.

You can't even breathe. Mercury has no air.

No one has ever seen the other side of Mercury.

Mercury is the planet closest to the Sun.

Mercury is the smallest planet in the **solar system**.

Mercury

Sun

9

The side of the planet that faces the Sun is boiling hot.

The side that faces away from the Sun is freezing cold.

Mercury is only 36 million miles from the Sun.

Mercury is made mostly of iron.

It has a very big **core** for such a little planet.

Scientists think part of the core is made of liquid iron.

core

crust

13

Mercury looks like Earth's **moon**.

Mercury and the Moon both have many **craters**.

Most of the craters were made millions of years ago.

Many of the craters were made by **meteorites**.

meteorite

crater on
Mercury

crater on
Earth's moon

15

One of the largest craters on Mercury is called the Caloris Basin.

It was made by an asteroid, a large rocky object, that hit Mercury.

The entire state of Texas could fit inside the Caloris Basin.

Rim of the
Caloris Basin

Scientists know some facts about Mercury because of a **space probe** called *Mariner 10*.

In 1975, *Mariner 10* finished its job.

Another space probe, *MESSENGER*, will arrive near Mercury in 2011.

You cannot go to Mercury. Aren't you glad that space probes can?

MESSENGER

A space probe does not carry people.

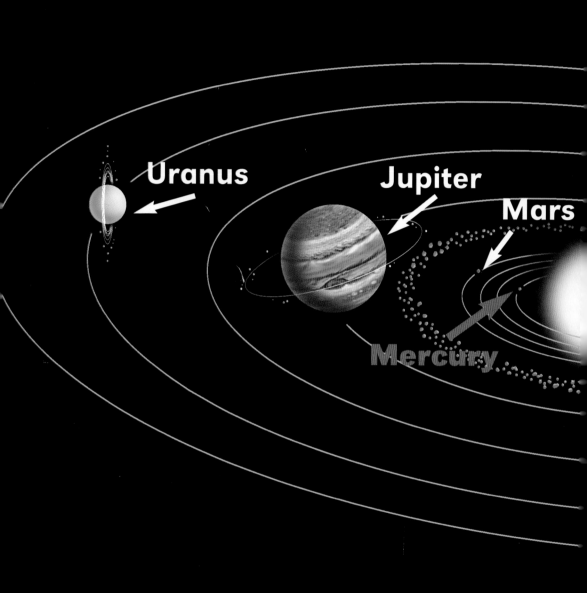

Uranus

Jupiter

Mars

Mercury

20

MERCURY

IN OUR SOLAR SYSTEM

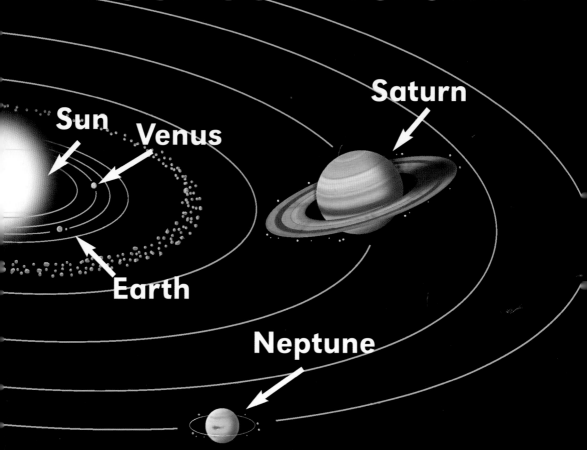

Sun

Venus

Saturn

Earth

Neptune

YOUR NEW WORDS

core (kor) the inside of an object

craters (**kray**-turz) large dents or holes in an object

Mercury (**muhr**-kyur-ree) a planet named after the Roman messenger of the gods

meteorite (**mee**-tee-ur-ite) a rock made of metal and stone that comes from outer space and lands on a planet or moon

moon (moon) an object that circles a planet

solar system (**soh**-lur **siss**-tuhm) the group of planets, moons, and other things that travel around the Sun

space probe (spayss prohb) a vehicle with robotic equipment used to explore space

Earth and Mercury

A year is how long it takes a planet to go around the Sun.

 1 Earth year =365 days

 1 Mercury year =88 Earth days

A day is how long it takes a planet to turn one time.

 1 Earth day = 24 hours

 1 Mercury day = 1,408 Earth hours

A moon is an object that circles a planet.

 Earth has 1 moon.

 Mercury has no moons.

The Sun can rise on Mercury two times in one day.

INDEX

FIND OUT MORE

Book:
Burnham, Robert. *Children's Atlas of the Universe*. Pleasantville, NY: Reader's Digest Children's Publishing, Inc., 2000.

Web site:
Solar System Exploration
http://sse.jpl.nasa.gov/planets

MEET THE AUTHOR

Christine Taylor-Butler is the author of more than twenty books for children. She holds a degree in Engineering from M.I.T. She lives in Kansas City with her family, where they have a telescope for searching the skies.

SCHOLASTIC

News

Nonfiction Readers

Mars

by
Melanie Chrismer

Children's Press
An Imprint of Scholastic Inc.
New York Toronto London Auckland Sydney
Mexico City New Delhi Hong Kong
Danbury, Connecticut

These content vocabulary word builders
are for grades 1–2.

Consultant: Michelle Yehling, Astronomy Education Consultant

Photo Credits:

Photographs © 2008: Corbis Images/Roger Ressmeyer: 4 top, 5 bottom left, 5 top left, 10, 13, 17; Getty Images: 5 bottom right, 6 (Ryan McVay), 4 bottom right, 9 (Antonio M. Rosario); NASA: cover (via SODA), back cover, 1, 4 bottom left, 5 top right, 11, 15, 23 right; Photo Researchers, NY: 7 (Rev. Ronald Royer), 2, 19 (Detlev van Ravenswaay); PhotoDisc/via SODA: 23 left.

Illustration Credit:

Illustration pages 20–21 by Greg Harris

Book Design: SimonSays Design!
Book Production: The Design Lab

Library of Congress Cataloging-in-Publication Data
Chrismer, Melanie.
Mars / by Melanie Chrismer.—Updated ed.
    p. cm.—(Scholastic news nonfiction readers)
Includes bibliographical references and index.
ISBN-13: 978-0-531-22627-8
ISBN-10: 0-531-22627-1
1. Mars (Planet)—Juvenile literature. I. Title.
QB641.C52 2007
523.43—dc22   2006102769

1 2 3 4 5 6 7 8 9 10 R 17 16 15 14 13 12 11 10 09 08

CONTENTS

WORD HUNT

Look for these words as you read. They will be in **bold**.

astronaut
(**ass**-truh-nawt)

rover
(**roh**-ver)

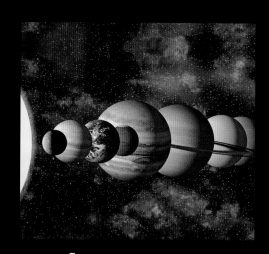

solar system
(**soh**-lur **siss**-tuhm)

4

astronomer
(uh-**stron**-uh-mur)

Mars
(mars)

space suit
(spayss soot)

telescope
(**tel**-uh-skope)

5

Mars!

There is a bright object in the night sky that is not a star.

It is the planet **Mars**!

You can see Mars without a **telescope**.

telescope

Mars

Stars are not the only bright objects in the night sky.

Mars is the fourth planet from the Sun.

The planets in our **solar system** travel around the Sun.

Mars is sometimes called the Red Planet because of its red soil.

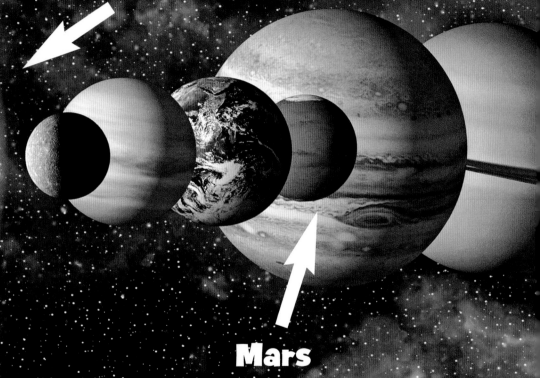

Sun

Mars

No person has gone to Mars.

Rovers have been put on Mars to explore it.

One day an **astronaut** may go to Mars.

astronaut

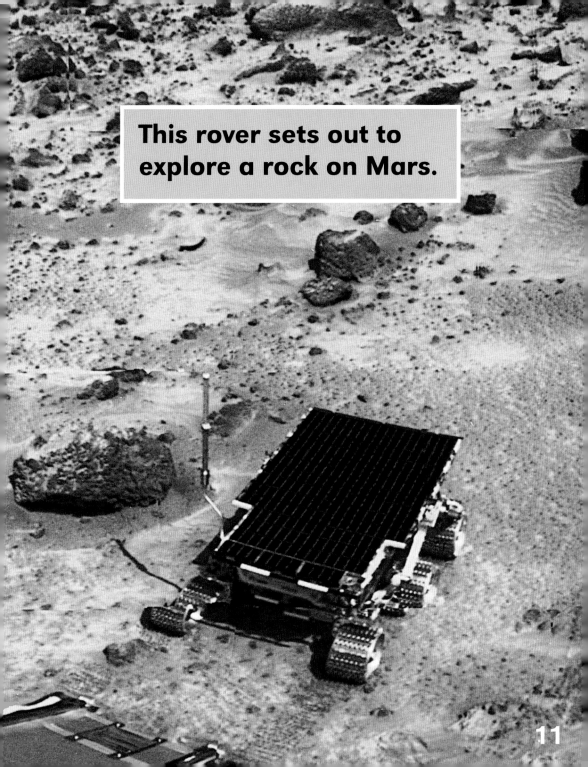

This rover sets out to explore a rock on Mars.

An **astronomer** is someone who studies stars, planets, and space.

Astronomers use telescopes and spacecraft to study Mars.

They are studying how people might live there one day.

We could fly to Mars in a spacecraft. It would take about eight months to get there!

Computers help astronomers gather information about space.

Mars has a North Pole and a South Pole, just like Earth.

There are giant sandstorms on Mars.

Mars has two moons.

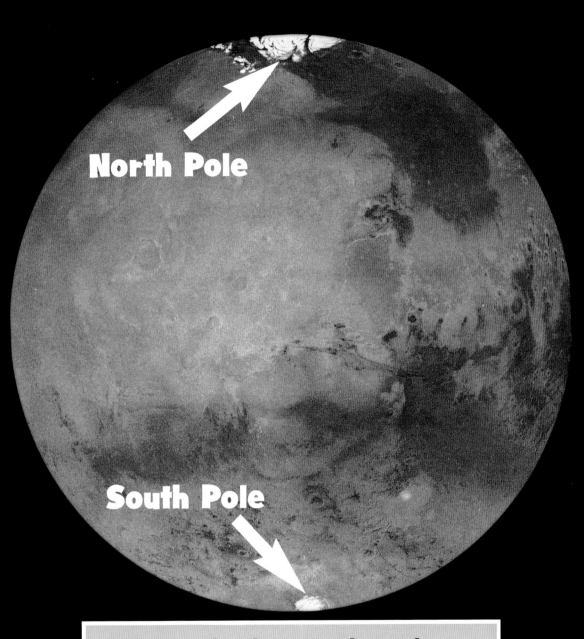

North Pole

South Pole

Like Earth, the North and South Poles on Mars have ice.

15

Mars is cold all the time.

Humans cannot breathe the air on Mars.

You would have to wear a **space suit** to breathe and stay warm on Mars.

Scientists are looking for signs of life on Mars.

They think people can live on Mars someday.

Do you want to live on Mars?

Is this what a city on Mars might look like?

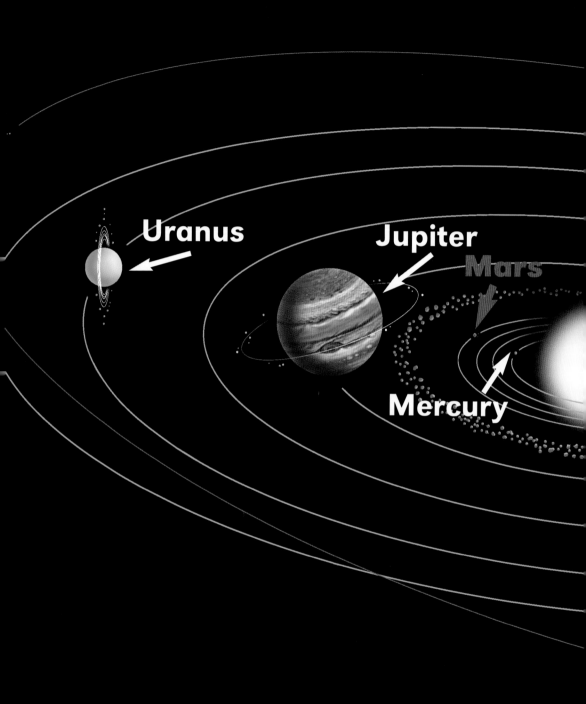

Uranus

Jupiter

Mars

Mercury

MARS

IN OUR SOLAR SYSTEM

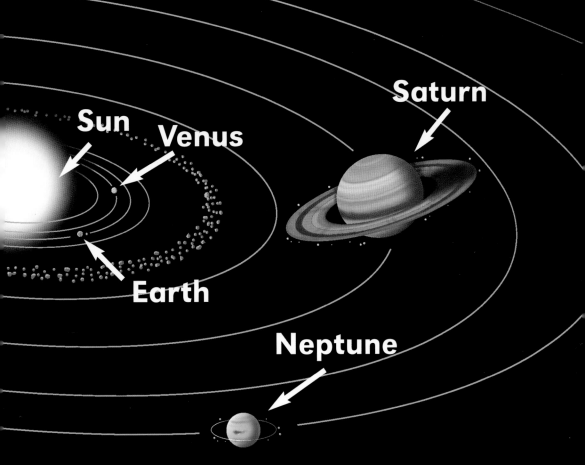

Sun

Venus

Saturn

Earth

Neptune

YOUR NEW WORDS

astronaut (**ass**-truh-nawt) a person trained to travel in space

astronomer (uh-**stron**-uh-mur) someone who studies stars, planets, and space

Mars (mars) a planet named after the Roman god of war

rover (**roh**-ver) a robot used to explore the surface of a planet or moon

solar system (**soh**-lur **siss**-tuhm) the group of planets, moons, and other things that travel around the Sun

space suit (spayss soot) special clothing to wear in space

telescope (**tel**-uh-skope) a tool used to see things far away

Earth and Mars

A year is how long it takes a planet to go around the Sun.

 **1 Earth year
=365 days**

 **1 Mars year
=687 Earth days**

A day is how long it takes a planet to turn one time.

 **1 Earth day
= 24 hours**

 **1 Mars day
= 24–25 Earth hours**

A moon is an object that circles a planet.

 **Earth has
1 moon.**

 **Mars has
2 moons.**

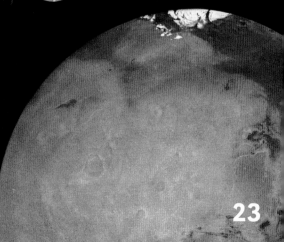

**Olympus Mons, the
biggest volcano on
Mars, is 3 times as tall
as Mount Everest.**

INDEX

FIND OUT MORE

Book:
Stille, Darlene R. *Mars*. Mankato, MN: Child's World, 2003.

Web site:
Solar System Exploration
http://sse.jpl.nasa.gov/planets/

MEET THE AUTHOR

Melanie Chrismer grew up near NASA in Houston, Texas. She loves math and science and has written thirteen books for children. To write her books, she visited NASA where she floated in the zero-gravity trainer called the Vomit Comet. She says, "it is the best roller coaster ever!"

Pluto
Dwarf Planet

by
Christine Taylor-Butler

Children's Press
An Imprint of Scholastic Inc.
New York Toronto London Auckland Sydney
Mexico City New Delhi Hong Kong
Danbury, Connecticut

These content vocabulary word builders
are for grades 1–2.

Consultant: Michelle Yehling, Astronomy Education Consultant

The image on the cover is an artist's rendition of Pluto.

Photo Credits:

Photographs © 2008: DK Images: 4 top, 13; NASA: 11 (John Hopkins University Applied Physics Laboratory/ Southwest Research Institute), 23 bottom (A. Schaller/ ESA), cover, 5 top right and bottom right, 10; Photo Researchers, NY: 2, 5 top left (Chris Butler), 1, 4 bottom right, 7 (Lynette Cook), back cover, 19 (Lynette Cook/SPL), 23 top (Mark Garlick), 15 (NASA/ESA/STScl), 5 bottom left, 9 (Deltev van Ravenswaay).

Illustration Credits:

Illustration pages 20–21 by Greg Harris   Illustrations page 4, 17 by Pat Rasch

Book Design: SimonSays Design!
Book Production: The Design Lab

Library of Congress Cataloging-in-Publication Data
Taylor-Butler, Christine.
Pluto : dwarf planet / By Christine Taylor-Butler.—Updated ed.
    p. cm.—(Scholastic news nonfiction readers)
Includes bibliographical references and index.
ISBN-13: 978-0-531-22630-8
ISBN-10: 0-531-22630-1
1. Pluto (Dwarf planet)—Juvenile literature. I. Title.
QB701.T39 2008
523.48'2—dc22   2006102779

1 2 3 4 5 6 7 8 9 10 R 17 16 15 14 13 12 11 10 09 08

CONTENTS

WORD HUNT

Look for these words as you read. They will be in **bold**.

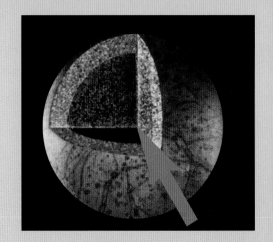

core
(kor)

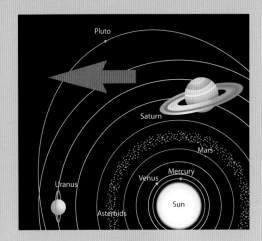

orbit
(**or**-bit)

Pluto
(**ploo**-toh)

moon
(moon)

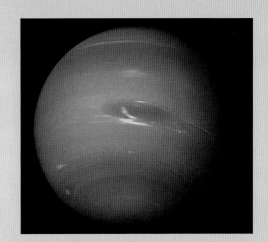

Neptune
(**nep**-toon)

solar system
(**soh**-lur **siss**-tuhm)

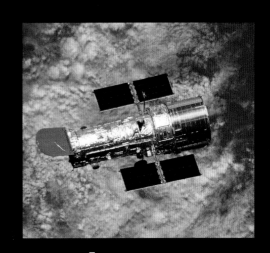

telescope
(**tel**-uh-skope)

Pluto!

Pluto is very far away.

Some pictures have been taken of Pluto. But in them, the surface of Pluto is hard to see.

Many pictures of Pluto are painted by artists.

An artist drew this picture of Pluto.

Pluto is a dwarf planet.

Dwarf planets are round like planets. But they are smaller. The space around them is full of smaller objects.

The area around planets is mostly empty.

Both planets and dwarf planets are found in the **solar system**.

Pluto

Sun

Pluto is farther from the Sun than all the planets.

It is hard to see even with a giant space **telescope**.

In 2006, a spaceship called *New Horizons* left for Pluto. It won't arrive until 2015!

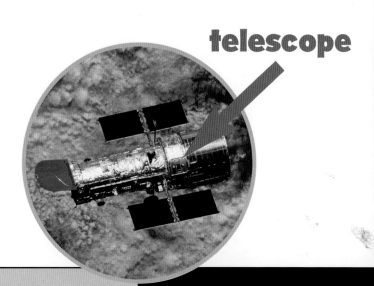

telescope

There are no people aboard *New Horizons*.

Scientists know that Pluto is made of both rock and ice.

The outside of Pluto is mostly solid ice.

The inside is called the **core**.

Scientists are not sure how much of the core is rock or ice.

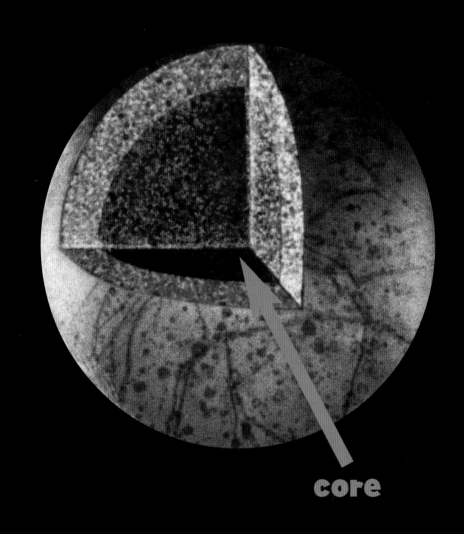

core

Earth has one **moon**. Pluto has three.

They are called Charon, Hydra, and Nix.

Charon and Pluto look alike. They both look like icy balls, but Charon is smaller than Pluto.

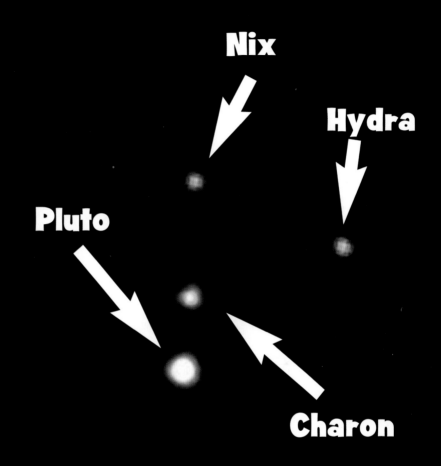

Nix

Hydra

Pluto

Charon

Charon is about half the size of Pluto.

Pluto goes around the Sun on a path called an **orbit**.

Pluto's path is shaped more like an oval than most planets' orbits.

Sometimes Pluto's orbit crosses **Neptune's** orbit. But Pluto and Neptune will never hit each other.

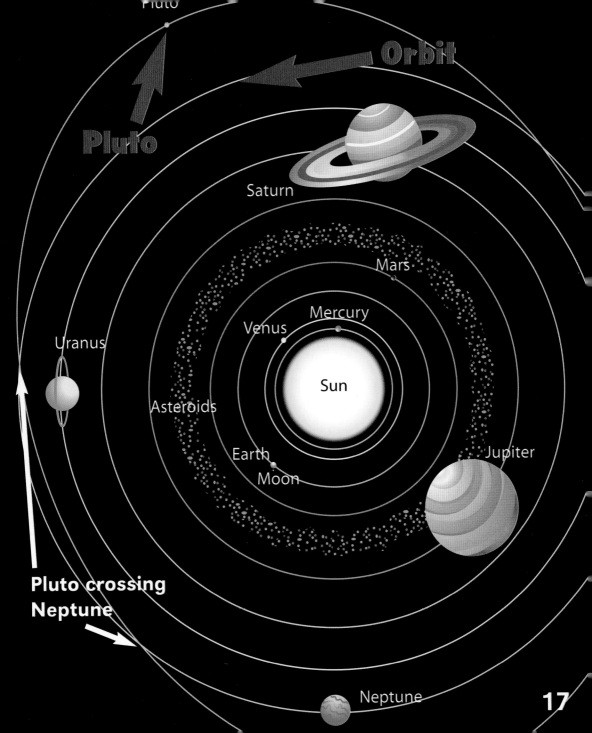

Pluto

Orbit

Pluto

Saturn

Mars

Venus Mercury

Uranus

Sun

Asteroids

Earth

Moon

Jupiter

Pluto crossing Neptune

Neptune

17

In 2226, Pluto will cross Neptune's orbit.

But Pluto will still be far away.

From the surface of Pluto, the Sun will still look as small as a star.

Will we know what Pluto really looks like by 2226?

Maybe!

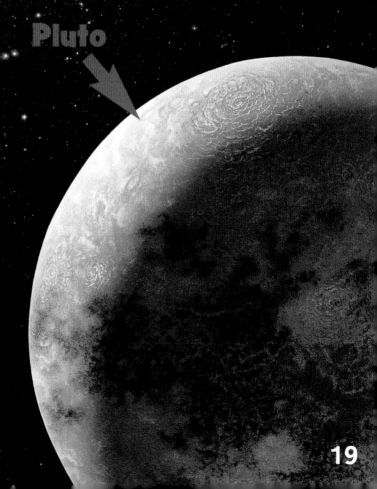

Sun

Pluto

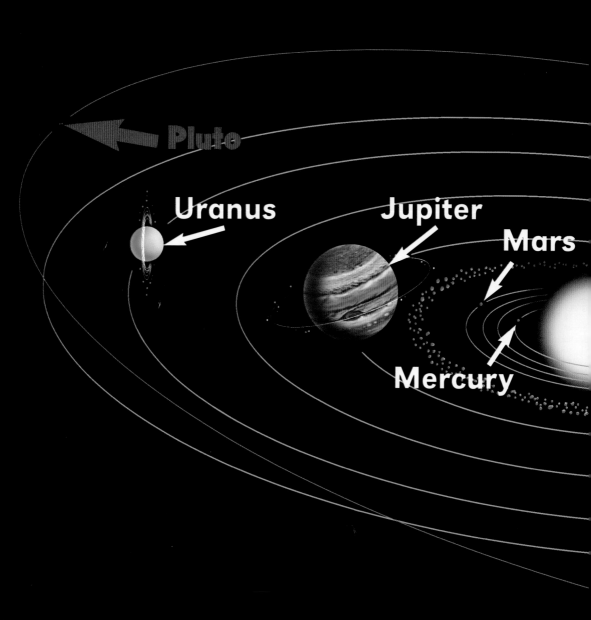

Pluto

Uranus

Jupiter

Mars

Mercury

PLUTO

IN OUR SOLAR SYSTEM

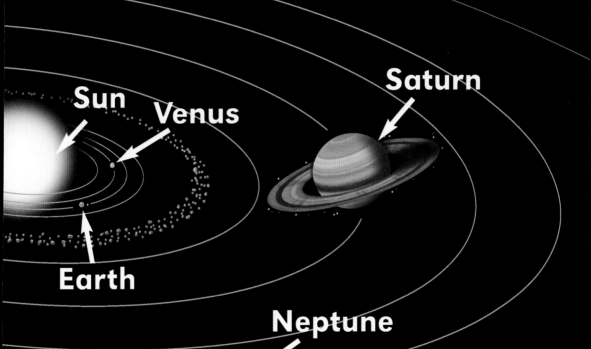

Saturn

Sun

Venus

Earth

Neptune

YOUR NEW WORDS

core (kor) the inside of an object

moon (moon) an object that
   circles a larger object

Neptune (**nep**-toon) a planet named after
   the Roman god of the sea

orbit (**or**-bit) the path an object takes
   around another object

Pluto (**ploo**-toh) a dwarf planet
   named after the Roman god of
   the underworld

solar system (**soh**-lur **siss**-tuhm) the
   group of planets, dwarf planets,
   moons, and other things that travel
   around the Sun

telescope (**tel**-uh-skope) a tool used to
   see things far away

Other Dwarf Planets

Ceres is found in an area between Mars and Jupiter called the Asteroid Belt.

Eris is in the Kuiper Belt, a ring of icy rocks outside the orbit of Neptune.

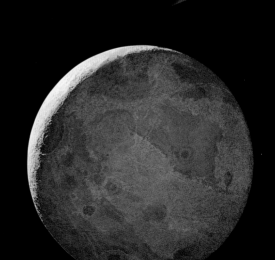

INDEX

FIND OUT MORE

Book:

Burnham, Robert. *Children's Atlas of the Universe.* Pleasantville, NY: Reader's Digest Children's Publishing, Inc., 2000.

Web site:

Solar System Exploration
http://sse.jpl.nasa.gov/planets

MEET THE AUTHOR

Christine Taylor-Butler is the author of more than twenty books for children. She holds a degree in Engineering from M.I.T. She lives in Kansas City with her family, where they have a telescope for searching the skies.

Venus

by
Melanie Chrismer

Children's Press
An Imprint of Scholastic Inc.
New York Toronto London Auckland Sydney
Mexico City New Delhi Hong Kong
Danbury, Connecticut

These content vocabulary word builders
are for grades 1–2.

Consultant: Michelle Yehling, Astronomy Education Consultant

Photo Credits:

Photographs © 2008: Corbis Images: 19 (Wolfgang Kaehler), 7 (Roy Morsch), 4 bottom left, 15 top (Galen Rowell); NASA: 5 top left, 5 top right, 15 bottom; Peter Arnold Inc./Astrofoto: back cover, 5 bottom left, 9; Photo Researchers, NY: 4 top, 11 top (European Space Agency/SPL), 13 (Mark Marten/NASA), 1, 2, 5 bottom right, 11 bottom, 23 right (NASA/Science Source); PhotoDisc/Getty Images via SODA: cover, 17, 23 left.

Illustration Credits:

Illustration page 4 bottom right by Pat Rasch

Illustration pages 20–21 by Greg Harris

Book Design: SimonSays Design!
Book Production: The Design Lab

Library of Congress Cataloging-in-Publication Data
Chrismer, Melanie.
Venus / by Melanie Chrismer.—Updated ed.
 p. cm.—(Scholastic news nonfiction readers)
Includes bibliographical references and index.
ISBN-13: 978-0-531-22633-9
ISBN-10: 0-531-22633-6
1. Venus (Planet)—Juvenile literature. I. Title.
QB621.C57 2007
523.42—dc22   2006102780

1 2 3 4 5 6 7 8 9 10 R   17 16 15 14 13 12 11 10 09 08

CONTENTS

WORD HUNT

Look for these words as you read. They will be in **bold**.

clouds
(kloudz)

mountains
(**moun**-tuhnz)

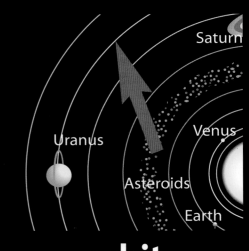

orbit
(**or**-bit)

Saturn

Uranus

Venus

Asteroids

Earth

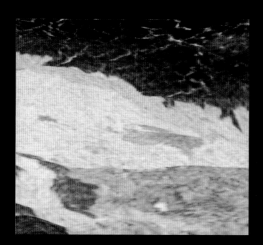

lava
(**lah**-vuh)

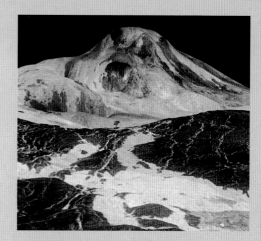

Maat Mons
(maht monz)

solar system
(**soh**-lur **siss**-tuhm)

Venus
(**vee**-nuhs)

Venus!

It is fun to fly a kite on Earth.

But can you go fly a kite on **Venus**?

No. You cannot go to Venus at all.

Flying kites on Earth is fun.

Venus is the second planet in our **solar system**.

All of the planets in the solar system travel around the Sun on a path called an **orbit**.

Venus is closer to the Sun than Earth is. It is hotter on Venus than on Earth.

Venus

Earth

9

Venus is called Earth's sister. They are the same in many ways.

They are almost the same size.

They are both made out of rock and metal.

They both have **clouds**.

Earth

Venus

Venus and Earth are different, too.

The clouds on Earth are made of water.

The clouds on Venus are made of acid.

The acid in the clouds on Venus would burn your skin.

Venus and Earth have **mountains** and volcanoes.

The highest mountain on Earth is Mount Everest.

The highest mountain on Venus is Maxwell Montes. It is almost 7 miles (11.5 kilometers) high.

One of the highest volcanoes on Venus is **Maat Mons**.

The highest volcano on Earth is Ojos del Salado. It is more than 4 miles (6.5 km) high.

Mount Everest is 5 1/2 miles (9 km) high.

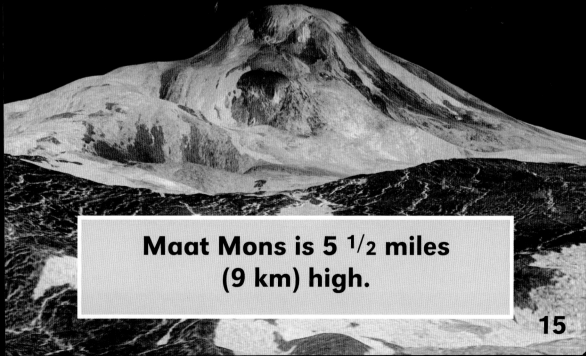

Maat Mons is 5 1/2 miles (9 km) high.

15

Almost all of Venus is covered with **lava**. Lava is hot melted rock or melted rock that has cooled and hardened.

Almost all of Earth is covered with water.

oceans

17

No, you cannot fly a kite on Venus.

But on Earth you can do many things.

You can fly a kite. You can swim in the ocean, and you can be happy you do not live on Venus!

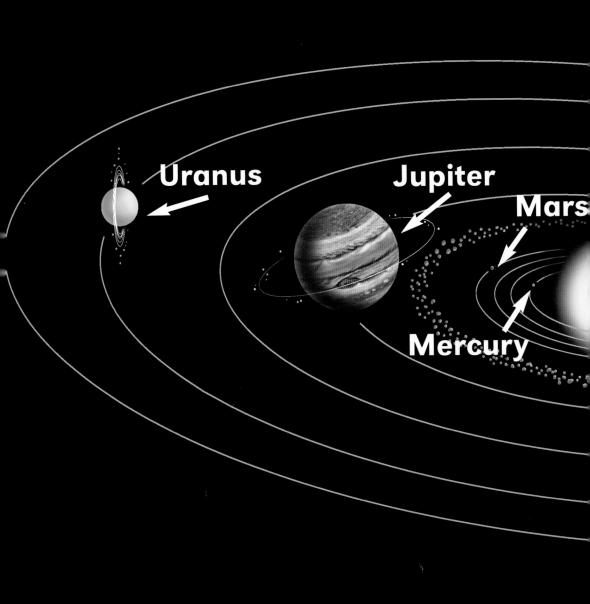

Uranus Jupiter Mars Mercury

VENUS

IN OUR SOLAR SYSTEM

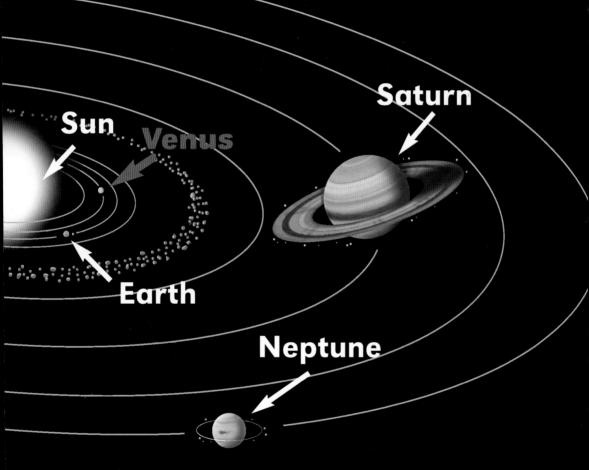

Sun

Venus

Earth

Saturn

Neptune

YOUR NEW WORDS

clouds (kloudz) groups of liquid droplets that can be seen above the surface of a planet

lava (**lah**-vuh) hot melted rock or melted rock that has cooled and hardened

Maat Mons (maht monz) one of the highest volcanoes on Venus

mountains (**moun**-tuhnz) high pieces of land

orbit (**or**-bit) the path an object takes around another object

solar system (**soh**-lur **siss**-tuhm) the group of planets, moons, and other things that travel around the Sun

Venus (**vee**-nuhs) a planet named after the Roman goddess of beauty and love

Earth and Venus

A year is how long it takes a planet to go around the Sun.

 1 Earth year =365 days

 1 Venus year =225 Earth days

A day is how long it takes a planet to turn one time.

 1 Earth day = 24 hours

 1 Venus day = 5,834 Earth hours or 243 Earth days

A moon is an object that circles a planet.

 Earth has 1 moon.

 Venus has no moons.

Astronomers have found a lava river on Venus that is more than 4,000 miles (6,437 km) long.

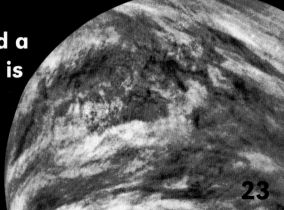

INDEX

FIND OUT MORE

Book:

Cole, Michael D. *Venus: The Second Planet*. Berkeley Heights, NJ: Enslow Publishers, Inc., 2001.

Web site:

Solar System Exploration
http://sse.jpl.nasa.gov/planets/

MEET THE AUTHOR

Melanie Chrismer grew up near NASA in Houston, Texas. She loves math and science and has written thirteen books for children. To write her books, she visited NASA where she floated in the zero-gravity trainer called the Vomit Comet. She says, "it is the best roller coaster ever!"

SCHOLASTIC
News
Nonfiction Readers

Neptune

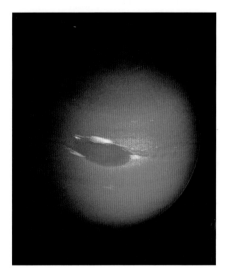

by
Melanie Chrismer

Children's Press
An Imprint of Scholastic Inc.
New York Toronto London Auckland Sydney
Mexico City New Delhi Hong Kong
Danbury, Connecticut

These content vocabulary word builders
are for grades 1–2.

Consultant: Michelle Yehling, Astronomy Education Consultant

Photo Credits:

Photographs © 2008: Bridgeman Art Library International Ltd., London/New York: 17 top (Lauros/Giraudon/Chateau de Versailles, France, by Felix Henri Giacomotti); Corbis Images/Hulton-Deutsch Collection: 17 bottom; NASA: back cover (JPL), cover, 2, 4 top, 5 bottom right, 5 top left, 7, 11, 19, 23 right; Photo Researchers, NY: 4 bottom right, 9 (Detlev van Ravenswaay), 4 bottom left, 5 bottom left, 15 (SPL); PhotoDisc/Getty Images via SODA: 1, 23 left, 23 top left.

Illustration Credits:

Illustration pages 5 top right, 13 by Pat Rasch   Illustrations on pages 20–21 by Greg Harris

Book Design: SimonSays Design!
Book Production: The Design Lab

Library of Congress Cataloging-in-Publication Data
Chrismer, Melanie.
Neptune / by Melanie Chrismer.—Updated ed.
    p. cm.—(Scholastic news nonfiction readers)
Includes bibliographical references and index.
ISBN-13: 978-0-531-22629-2
ISBN-10: 0-531-22629-8
1. Neptune (Planet)—Juvenile literature. I. Title.
QB691.C48 2007
523.48'1—dc22   2006102772

1 2 3 4 5 6 7 8 9 10 R 17 16 15 14 13 12 11 10 09 08

CONTENTS

WORD HUNT

Look for these words as you read. They will be in **bold**.

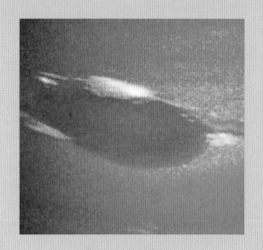

clouds
(kloudz)

scientists
(**sye**-uhn-tists)

solar system
(**soh**-lur **siss**-tuhm)

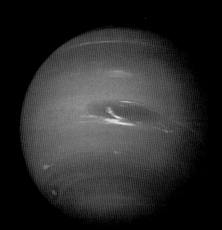

Neptune
(**nep**-toon)

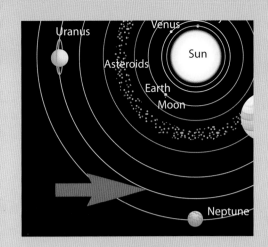

orbit
(**or**-bit)

telescope
(**tel**-uh-skope)

Uranus
(**yu**-rah-nuhss)

5

Neptune!

The planet **Neptune** looks blue.

It was named after Neptune, the Roman god of the sea.

Is there a sea of blue water on Neptune?

No. The blue color comes from the gas around the planet.

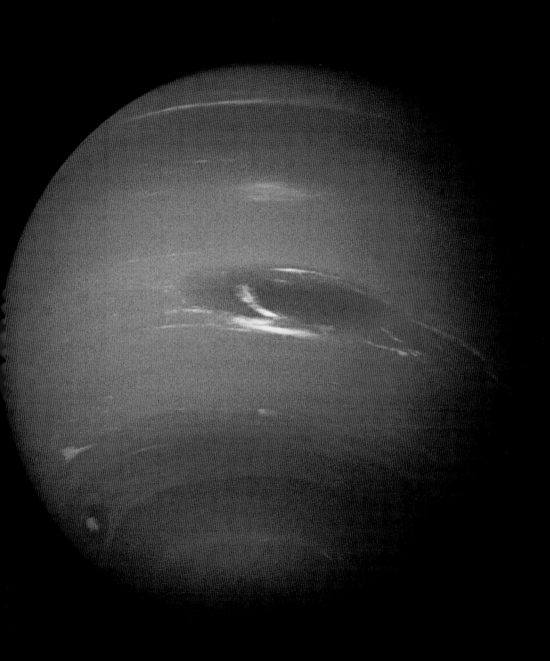

There is no water on Neptune.

Neptune is one of the biggest planets in our **solar system**.

Neptune is the eighth planet in our solar system.

All the planets in our solar system travel around the Sun on a path called an **orbit**.

Neptune

Uranus

Jupiter

Earth

9

Neptune is a big, cold, cloudy, windy planet.

Its **clouds** are made of a gas called methane.

Neptune also has the fastest winds of all the planets.

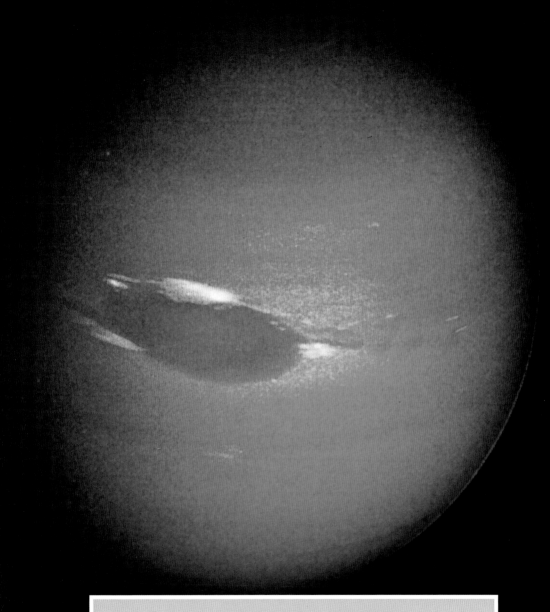

In some pictures of Neptune, its clouds look pink.

Before **scientists** found Neptune, they were studying the planet **Uranus**.

They were surprised by its orbit.

Uranus did not follow the path they thought it would.

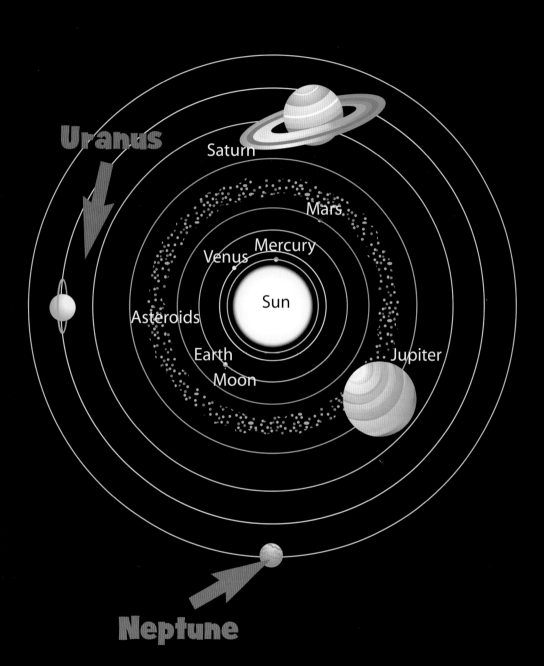

Uranus

Saturn

Mars

Mercury

Venus

Sun

Asteroids

Earth

Moon

Jupiter

Neptune

13

Scientists thought another planet was causing Uranus to travel in an unusual orbit.

They used math to figure out where the other planet might be.

Then astronomers used a **telescope** to look for it.

Telescopes are used to
see things far away.

In 1846 the astronomers found the planet they were looking for.

They named it Neptune after the Roman god of the sea.

Urbain Le Verrier (top) and John Couch Adams (bottom) did the math to help discover Neptune.

Neptune was the first planet found using math.

Most of the other planets were found by watching the sky.

Who knows what other wonderful things will be found in space?

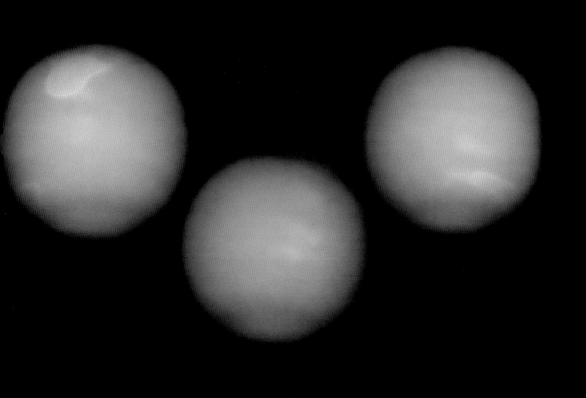

These pictures of Neptune were taken from the Hubble Space Telescope.

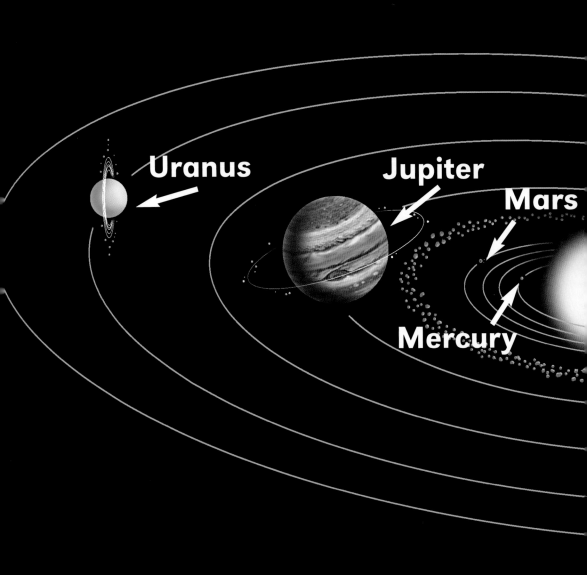

Uranus

Jupiter

Mars

Mercury

NEPTUNE
IN OUR SOLAR SYSTEM

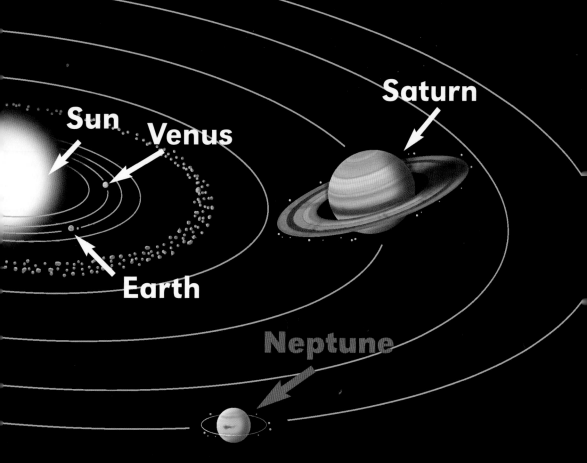

Sun

Venus

Saturn

Earth

Neptune

YOUR NEW WORDS

clouds (kloudz) groups of liquid droplets that can be seen above the surface of a planet

Neptune (**nep**-toon) a planet named after the Roman god of the sea

orbit (**or**-bit) the path an object takes around another object

scientists (**sye**-uhn-tists) people who study a subject by testing and observing

solar system (**soh**-lur **siss**-tuhm) the group of planets, moons, and other things that travel around the Sun

telescope (**tel**-uh-skope) a tool used to see things far away

Uranus (**yu**-rah-nuhss) the seventh planet

Earth and Neptune

A year is how long it takes a planet to go around the Sun.

 **1 Earth year
=365 days**

 **1 Neptune year
=60,225 Earth days
or 165 Earth years**

A day is how long it takes a planet to turn one time.

 **1 Earth day
= 24 hours**

 **1 Neptune day
= 16 Earth hours**

A moon is an object that circles a planet.

 **Earth has
1 moon.**

 **Neptune has
at least 13 moons
with more being
found all the time.**

**The winds on Neptune
can blow more than 1,200
miles (1,931 kilometers)
per hour.**

INDEX

FIND OUT MORE

Book:

Jenkins, Alvin. *Next Stop Neptune: Experiencing the Solar System.* Boston: Houghton Mifflin, 2004.

Web site:

Solar System Exploration
http://sse.jpl.nasa.gov/planets/

MEET THE AUTHOR

Melanie Chrismer grew up near NASA in Houston, Texas. She loves math and science and has written thirteen books for children. To write her books, she visited NASA where she floated in the zero-gravity trainer called the Vomit Comet. She says, "it is the best roller coaster ever!"

SCHOLASTIC
News
Nonfiction Readers

Saturn

by
Christine Taylor-Butler

Children's Press
An Imprint of Scholastic Inc.
New York Toronto London Auckland Sydney
Mexico City New Delhi Hong Kong
Danbury, Connecticut

These content vocabulary word builders
are for grades 1–2.

Consultant: Michelle Yehling, Astronomy Education Consultant

Photo Credits:

Photographs © 2008: Corbis Images/Jim Zuckerman: 5 bottom right, 16; Finley Holiday Film: back cover; Getty Images/Antonio M. Rosario/The Image Bank: 4 bottom right, 13; NASA: 5 bottom left, 5 top right (Jet Propulsion Lab Photo), 9, 11, 17 (JPL/Space Science Institute), cover, 1, 4 bottom left, 7, 19, 23 right; Photo Researchers, NY: 2, 4 top, 15 (Lynette Cook/SPL); PhotoDisc/Getty Images via SODA: 23 left.

Illustration Credit:

Illustration pages 5 top left, 20–21 by Greg Harris

Book Design: SimonSays Design!
Book Production: The Design Lab

Library of Congress Cataloging-in-Publication Data
Taylor-Butler, Christine.
Saturn / by Christine Taylor-Butler.—Updated ed.
   p. cm.—(Scholastic news nonfiction readers)
Includes bibliographical references and index.
ISBN-13: 978-0-531-22631-5
ISBN-10: 0-531-22631-X
1. Saturn (Planet)—Juvenile literature. I. Title.
QB671.T235 2007
523.46—dc22   2006102773

1 2 3 4 5 6 7 8 9 10 R 17 16 15 14 13 12 11 10 09 08

CONTENTS

WORD HUNT

Look for these words as you read. They will be in **bold**.

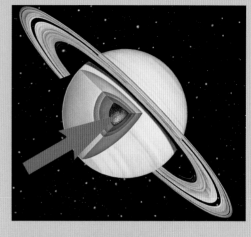

core
(kor)

Saturn
(**sat**-urn)

solar system
(**soh**-lur **siss**-tuhm)

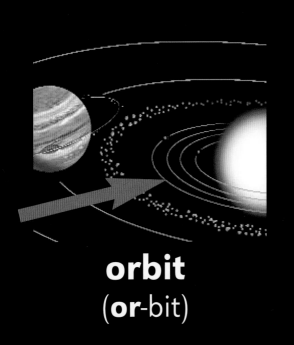

orbit
(**or**-bit)

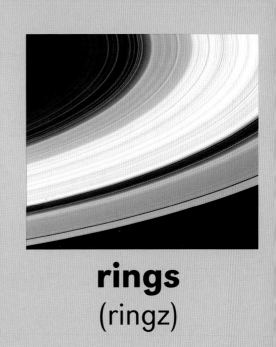

rings
(ringz)

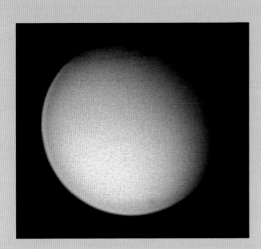

Titan
(**tie**-tuhn)

tornado
(tor-**nay**-doh)

Saturn!

Saturn has **rings**.

The rings **orbit**, or travel around, the planet.

There is ice in Saturn's rings.

Can you skate on Saturn's rings? No.

The rings are not one solid piece. There is ice but also dust, rock, and empty space, too.

Other planets also have rings.

But Saturn has the most rings.

Scientists think there are 10,000 rings or more around Saturn.

Saturn's rings are very wide and very flat.

There are at least 56 moons that orbit Saturn.

The largest moon is **Titan**.

It has an atmosphere and clouds. An atmosphere is the gas that surrounds an object in space.

Titan was discovered in 1655.

Saturn is the sixth planet from the Sun.

Saturn is the second largest planet in the **solar system**.

All the planets in the solar system orbit the Sun.

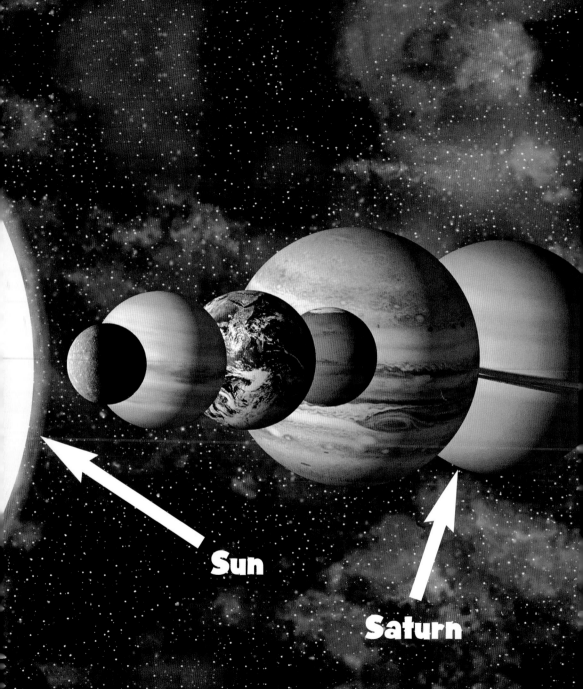

Sun

Saturn

Saturn is a giant ball of gas.

Deep inside the planet the gas becomes a hot liquid.

At the very middle of the planet is the **core**. The core is made mostly of rock.

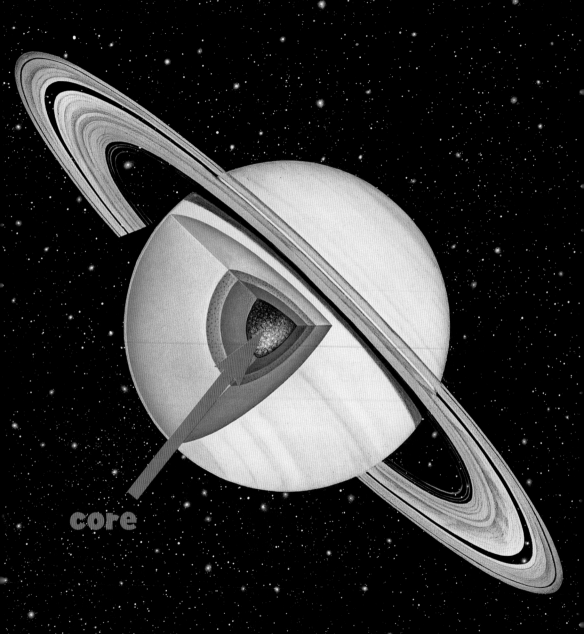

core

15

On Saturn, the wind blows very fast.

Sometimes the wind blows 1,100 miles per hour.

That is more than five times faster than the winds inside a **tornado** on Earth!

tornado

Saturn is very big,
but it is one of the
lightest planets.

One of the gases it
is made of is helium.

That's the gas that
makes balloons float!

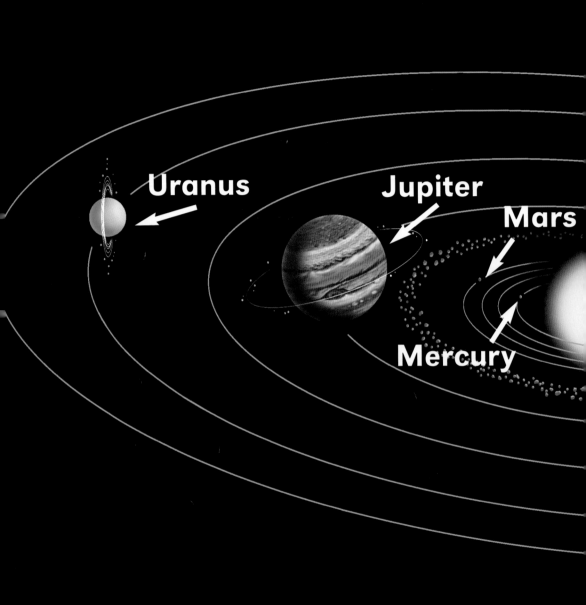

Uranus

Jupiter

Mars

Mercury

SATURN
IN OUR SOLAR SYSTEM

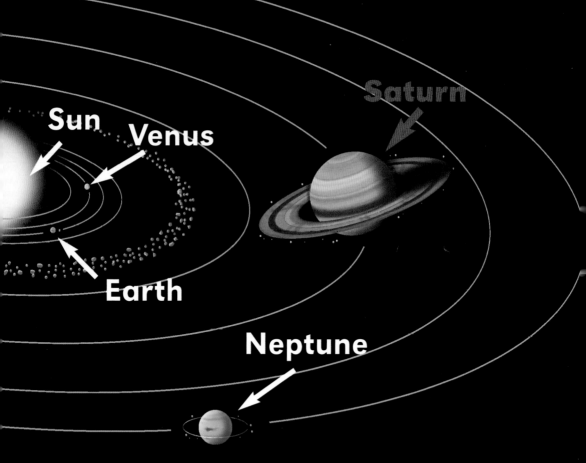

Sun

Venus

Earth

Saturn

Neptune

YOUR NEW WORDS

core (kor) the inside of an object

orbit (**or**-bit) to travel around a planet or the Sun

rings (ringz) bands of rocks, dust, and ice that circle a planet

Saturn (**sat**-urn) a planet named after the Roman god of the harvest

solar system (**soh**-lur **siss**-tuhm) the group of planets, moons, and other things that travel around the Sun

Titan (**tie**-tuhn) the largest moon of Saturn

tornado (tor-**nay**-doh) a funnel-shaped windstorm

Earth and Saturn

A year is how long it takes a planet to go around the Sun.

 1 Earth year =365 days

 1 Saturn year =10,756 Earth days

A day is how long it takes a planet to turn one time.

 1 Earth day = 24 hours

 1 Saturn day = 11 Earth hours

A moon is a big rock that circles a planet.

 Earth has 1 moon.

 Saturn has 56 moons with more being found all the time.

You can fit about 764 Earths inside of Saturn.

INDEX

FIND OUT MORE
Book:
Burnham, Robert. *Children's Atlas of the Universe.* Pleasantville, NY: Reader's Digest Children's Publishing, Inc., 2000.

Web site:
Solar System Exploration
http://sse.jpl.nasa.gov/planets

MEET THE AUTHOR

Christine Taylor-Butler is the author of more than twenty books for children. She holds a degree in Engineering from M.I.T. She lives in Kansas City with her family, where they have a telescope for searching the skies.

SCHOLASTIC

News

Nonfiction Readers

Jupiter

by
Christine Taylor-Butler

Children's Press
An Imprint of Scholastic Inc.
New York Toronto London Auckland Sydney
Mexico City New Delhi Hong Kong
Danbury, Connecticut

These content vocabulary word
builders are for grades 1–2.

Consultant: Michelle Yehling, Astronomy Education Consultant

Photo Credits:

Photographs © 2008: Finley Holiday Films: cover, 2, 4 bottom left, 7, 23; Holiday Film Corp.: 5 bottom right, 13; NASA: back cover, 1, 4 top, 5 top left, 5 top right, 5 bottom left, 9, 15, 17, 19; Photo Researchers, NY/Detlev van Ravenswaay: 4 bottom right, 11; PhotoDisc/Getty Images via SODA: 23 spot art.

Illustration Credit:

Illustration pages 20–21 by Greg Harris.

Book Design: SimonSays Design!
Book Production: The Design Lab

Library of Congress Cataloging-in-Publication Data
Taylor-Butler, Christine.
Jupiter / by Christine Taylor-Butler.—Updated ed.
    p. cm.—(Scholastic news nonfiction readers)
Includes bibliographical references and index.
ISBN-13: 978-0-531-22626-1
ISBN-10: 0-531-22626-3
1. Jupiter (Planet)—Juvenile literature. I. Title.
QB661.T39 2007
523.45—dc22   2006102768

CONTENTS

WORD HUNT

Look for these words as you read. They will be in **bold**.

bands
(bandz)

Jupiter
(**joo**-pih-tuhr)

solar system
(**soh**-lur **siss**-tuhm)

4

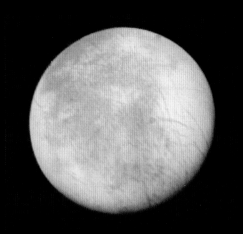

Europa
(yur-**oh**-pah)

Io
(**eye**-oh)

space probe
(spayss prohb)

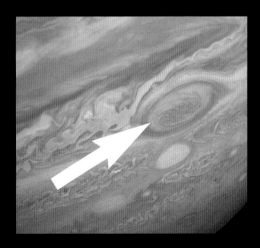

storm
(storm)

5

Jupiter!

Can you dance on **Jupiter**?

No. You cannot dance on Jupiter.

You cannot even stand on the planet.

Jupiter is made mostly of liquid and gas.

There are lots of clouds on Jupiter.

They make the planet look like it has stripes.

The clouds form **bands** of color. They are blue, brown, yellow, white, and red.

The bands move in opposite directions.

The wind in the bands blows very fast.

On Jupiter, winds have blown as fast as 400 miles (644 kilometers) per hour.

Jupiter is the fifth planet from the Sun.

It is the largest planet in the **solar system**.

You could fit more than 1,300 Earths inside Jupiter.

Jupiter

Earth

Sun

On Jupiter, there is a **storm** called the Great Red Spot.

This storm is two times wider than our whole planet.

This storm is like a hurricane on Earth. But it has lasted at least 340 years.

It is one of Jupiter's many storms.

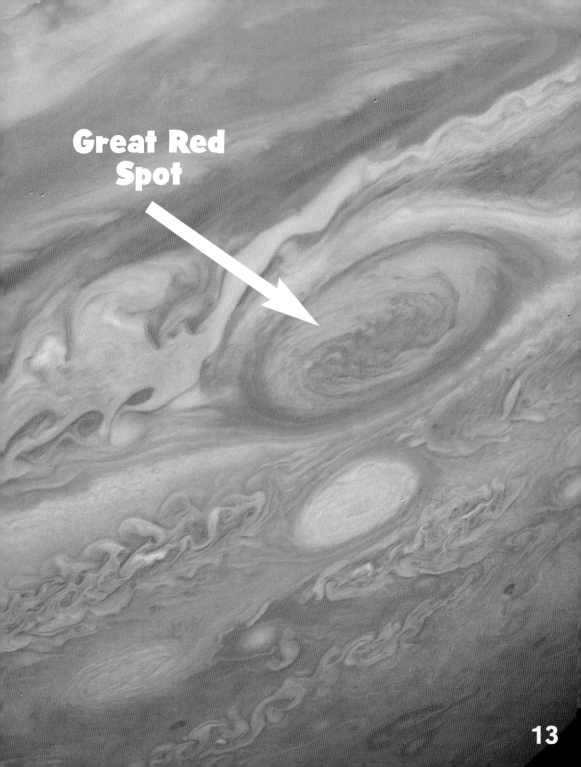

Great Red
Spot

Jupiter has more moons than any other planet.

It has at least 63 moons.

One of Jupiter's largest moons is **Io** (**eye**-oh).

Io has many volcanoes.

A volcano is a mountain made of lava. Lava is hot melted rock or melted rock that has cooled and hardened.

Io is about the same
size as Earth's moon.

Europa is another of Jupiter's largest moons.

This moon looks very different from Io.

It is covered with ice.

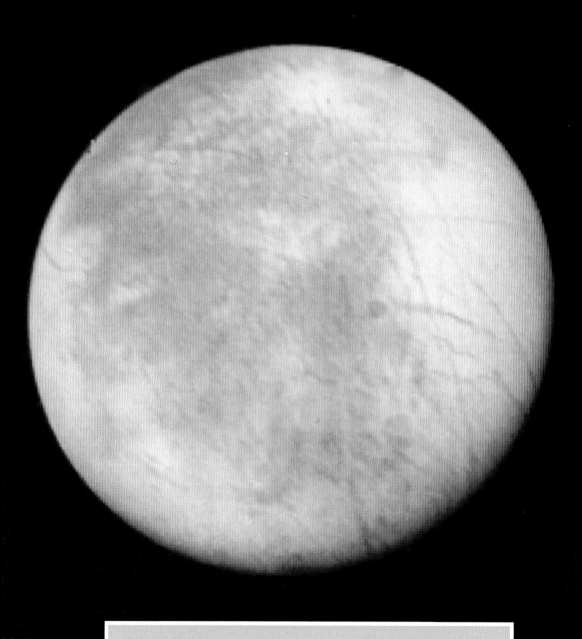

The layer of ice on Europa's surface is several miles thick.

The **space probe** *Galileo* went to Jupiter.

For almost eight years, it helped scientists learn about Jupiter's storms and moons.

In 2003 *Galileo* could do no more.

Scientists at NASA crashed it into Jupiter. They did not want it to hit any of Jupiter's moons.

A space probe has
no people in it.

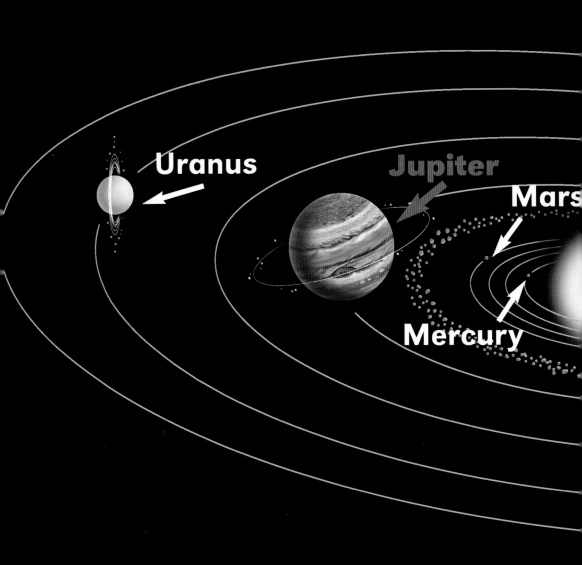

Uranus

Jupiter

Mars

Mercury

JUPITER
IN OUR SOLAR SYSTEM

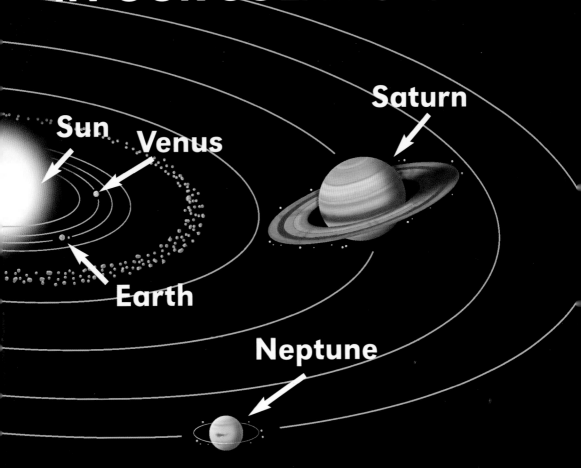

Saturn

Sun

Venus

Earth

Neptune

YOUR NEW WORDS

bands (bandz) long strips of clouds

Europa (yur-**oh**-pah) one of Jupiter's largest moons

Io (**eye**-oh) one of Jupiter's largest moons

Jupiter (**joo**-pih-tuhr) a planet named after the king of the Roman gods

solar system (**soh**-lur **siss**-tuhm) the group of planets, moons, and other things that travel around the Sun

space probe (spayss prohb) a vehicle with robotic equipment used to explore space

storm (storm) violent weather with strong winds

Earth and Jupiter

A year is how long it takes a planet to go around the Sun.

 1 Earth year =365 days

 1 Jupiter year =4,331 Earth days

A day is how long it takes a planet to turn one time.

 1 Earth day = 24 hours

 1 Jupiter day = 10 Earth hours

A moon is an object that circles a planet.

 Earth has 1 moon.

 Jupiter has 63 moons with more being found all the time.

Jupiter is the fastest turning planet in our solar system.

INDEX

FIND OUT MORE

Book:

Burnham, Robert. *Children's Atlas of the Universe.* Pleasantville, NY: Reader's Digest Children's Publishing, Inc., 2000.

Web site:

Solar System Exploration
http://sse.jpl.nasa.gov/planets

MEET THE AUTHOR

Christine Taylor-Butler is the author of more than twenty books for children. She holds a degree in Engineering from M.I.T. She lives in Kansas City with her family, where they have a telescope for searching the skies.